Decide!

How to make any decision

Karen Okulicz

K-Slaw, Inc.
P.O. Box 375
Belmar, NJ 07719
www.OKULICZ.com

Published by K-Slaw, Inc
          P.O. Box 375
          Belmar, New Jersey 07719
          (888) 529-6090

Library of Congress Control Number: 2001117696

ISBN 13: 978-0-9644260-1-6

First Printing, October, 2001
Second Printing, June, 2002
Third Printing, June, 2003
Fourth Printing, April, 2004
Fifth Printing, May, 2005
Sixth Printing, February, 2008
Seventh Printing, April, 2009

Printed in the United States of America

To my niece and nephew

Claudia Katherine Okulicz
Christian Gabriel Okulicz

"Don't look in any one else's garden but your own."

Olga Schwenka Prostoff
Grandma

Table of Contents

Introduction

Decide! offers simple ways to get to a decision quickly and painlessly, eliminating unnecessary pondering and agonizing. You will learn techniques that will assist you in making a decision: movement, listing, asking, visualizing, recognizing the timing of things and being kind to yourself.

Please enjoy this book as I enjoyed the process of explaining some tangible and intangible concepts on how to make a decision.

Decide well!

1

To make our own best decisions, I am sure we agree we must have a clear mind. Right? Not a mind that is muddled and confused.

One of the best ways to have clear thinking is to exercise. (No screaming please! Don't throw the book. We have just begun.) I will mention other ways in a while, but the quickest way for clarity is to get the body moving. What does that have to do with the mind? If you haven't heard, the body and mind are connected. Not only are they housed in the same person, they work together moment to moment. It's simple: the good you do for your body affects your mind and vice versa.

Now that I have said the dreaded word...exercise, let me further explain. I am in no way saying go run marathons, or join an expensive gym with fancy gear. That is up to you. In fact, I am grateful today that exercise-wear is a very large T-shirt over a pair of leggings or shorts. The retirement of the mandatory leotard to me is a great advancement in society.

What I am saying is do something physical. Walk,

run if you must, bike, swim, garden or yoga. Do something that keeps you moving. We are all so different, one type of movement may not fit the personality of another.

Of course, when starting anything new in regards to exercise, if you have a medical condition, check with your doctor for a medical clearance. All others, off the couch.

It is a struggle to begin. It is very easy to make excuses not to move. It's too hot, it's rainy, too sunny, too windy or too cold. Hard to start and to maintain. But once you begin, like any habit, it becomes you. You get hooked. Hooked on the sport or exercise itself. Hooked on the benefits of the outcome that movement provides.

The outcome and the benefits far outweigh the excuses for not doing anything. To name a few benefits, other than clearing the mind...movement:

* alleviates stress
* assists with digestion

* conquers depression
* promotes confidence
* helps you sleep soundly
* strengthens the heart
* takes and keeps weight off
* decreases the chances of osteoporosis
* increases the better cholesterol (HDL) and decreases the bad cholesterol (LDL), and will absolutely give you more energy. Exercise will improve your breathing, your posture, and your skin tone. It will release those wonderful natural chemicals (endorphins) that make you feel so great. Enough said.

Another great thing that scientists have found is that you don't have to do your daily exercise in one session. The movement you do throughout the day is accumulative. So park that car away from your office building or grocery store, and walk in. Exercise will not guarantee a longer life, but you look and feel better while you are alive. Also, if you were to get sick, the activity of exercise will be an added benefit to a healing recovery. Like having health credits in the bank.

I love the saying "I get my ideas in the shower." I do.

Mostly, it's a shower right after doing a bit of something physical. Ideas just flow.

The mind has been relaxed to get some clear thoughts and creativity through the muck of the daily grind. The muck that layers up as you go through the day. The muck of the should-haves, could-haves, forgot-tos and maybe get-tos.

Being in the process of exercise also clears your mind. Let's say it's an outside walk. If by the beach, walking gives you the physical benefits and also the mental image of looking outside yourself. You can't help to. You see the birds, smell the salt air, see the sun glistening on the water. If you walk in a city you see the architecture of the buildings, window-shop as you pass stores, people-watch, smell the air for whatever it may bring you: a hot dog stand scent, the smell of the sun hitting concrete. If you walk in a neighborhood you look at homes and upkeep. Don't we? The observations of your terrain assist in clearing your mind.

The process of going to exercise and doing exercise can alter your mood. If you go to a gym and take classes, you know you are different after the class. Exercise almost tricks you into feeling better. You can't help but feel better. Plus, there is a socialization with exercise. You get out and intermingle with people. Even solo walking, the daily nod hello to another walker somehow is a comfort when all seems to be in chaos.

Exercise is something we can control. Very few things in life we have control over. We can set up a routine and make it a habit. We can also control the type, time and amount of movement.

How much or how little should you do? Well, by the time this book comes out, there will be one more study that will say a certain amount of exercise is beneficial, and how many times a week. This control is up to you. For the beginner, it is maybe as little as a mindful ten minutes of something new, that grows into a life-long lifestyle addition. For those of you who do exercise, and then don't—you know who you are—just get back to whatever it was you were doing, or try something new.

So grab the umbrella, it's raining and time for a walk.

2

Write It Out
To Right It Out

Walk finished. Now we have a clear mind. Simple as that. Don't I wish all things were that easy? Read it, it's done. No practice, no stumbles. Never having to be patient. Never having to wade through the volumes of daily input we receive via mail, phones, faxes, other people, e-mails, newspapers, TV and radio, to find ourselves. Not the way it is in this lifetime. Sorry.

The next step is "write it out, to right it out." What does that mean? Write it down. Make a list or write in a journal. Put it in black and white, or red crayon if you must. Look at yourself in the reflection of your writing. You are there. The most honest you is present. The private you comes forward, the you who is always right.

Keeping lists, or a journal, is a way to focus our thoughts. It can validate a view of life the way we want it to be, and list the ways we will achieve that wanting. It is a great source of control during stressful times. It keeps us on track, it keeps us centered. We can see our progress of where we are going, and where we have been. This process of "writing it out" assists in going forward one more step. As we all know, some days are a step at a time, and other days we merrily skip along.

There are as many types of lists as there are people, maybe ten times that. We have the lists of what to get at the grocery store, the lists of what type of home to buy, what type of work we are looking for, what kind of car to buy and options in it, or what kind of person we want to marry, or have a relationship with. I am sure you can add many more types.

The time frames of lists come in almost as many varieties. We can have the daily to-do list, let's say: Dentist at 2 PM, get milk, finish chapter two. A weekly list: schedule a haircut, call the vet, pick up the dry cleaning. A monthly list: have car tuned up, pay mortgage, arrange for future vacation. (Very nice.) A yearly list: purchase new car, change jobs, look to move, save so much. Sometimes a five-year-plan list.

Lists are great if you are feeling overwhelmed or something is bothering you. Write down what it is. It may be work, school, the marriage, the neighbors, the kids, the boss, etc., or just something is missing. Give details. I hate my boss because. I want out of the marriage because. I don't feel well: why? This would be a list of symptoms. Maybe at times it's just "all of it." All of your life is too much. Your life, right now, may be one full page or volumes of things that bother you, and need to be attended to. Believe me, when you start doing this technique, your lists will become shorter. This process assists us with making the journey through the daily input overload, to clear our minds and our lives.

It's helpful to do this before bed time. By letting go of "the bothers," and putting them on paper, you may have a better night's sleep. The bothers are still there, but they're on paper for review. Magically, the next morning somehow the list just doesn't look so bad.

You have control over doing the lists or not. Again, it is a way to unclutter your mind, to control and structure your time. An example of mind uncluttering: if you write down what needs to be done for the day, the nagging tape called "What do I have to do?" just doesn't loop as often. You've got it in writing. The mind is freer to think and explore other things.

Making a daily to-do list gives structure to your day. You can chart your efforts. Today I will send two resumes, get a birthday card, and call one ex-coworker. You know what needs to be done. During an unemployment time, a daily to-do list can be a life saver that shows accomplishments. You did send out two resumes, and called an ex-coworker. It's the accomplishment of doing something for yourself that will change the present situation of being without employment to being with. These accomplishments will get you the next employment. For those of you who have never been unemployed, you can't imagine the effort it takes to move through an unemployed day with grace. The same may be said for getting through a day gracefully when having an illness, raising children, or countless other stressful situations.

We may be listing life goals. Some people list life goals: of what will be wished for, or accomplished. Sometimes the big five-year plans look great on paper, but if you are not working on life daily, five years pass.

No accomplishment toward that goal or plan is made. A simple example: someone may say they want to open their own restaurant in five years. Are they going to school to learn how, or apprenticing? If the answer is no, I would bet in five years, no restaurant.

Goal-setting, list-making and decision-making for personal growth become almost impossible when you yourself are ill, or when you are caretaking for an ill loved one. If you are ill, you must have your wits about you just to keep up your health. A caretaker has the enormous responsibility of another person, plus yourself. When a loved one is ill, time just stops. This time is like being in a fog. That is usually how you're feeling, out of focus, as you visit your loved one in the hospital or clinic. This time in a fog, nothing seems real or familiar. I also refer to this time as "Styrofoam cup time," since that is exactly what we are eating and drinking out of during those hospital visits. Most of us face this type of time sooner or later. Some for others, and some for ourselves. This time is not forever, it just feels that way. If you are in a foggy Styrofoam cup time and you are reading this: be kind to yourself. You may not be able to attempt some of the techniques at the moment and some you may be able to incorporate with gusto.

By now you may have created a list of issues that need to be attended to. OK, now take the list and write a few solutions for each perceived problem to get you going in a direction for resolution. They are problems to you, annoyances. To someone else they are not problems. The saying "That's your problem" is really the truth.

Here is an example of a "morning anxiety list" I recently experienced, and how I dealt with it. I woke up to the car not working, flooding in the basement and needing upgrades to my computer software, pronto.

These items, written down, now look awfully superficial and silly to me, but that morning my mind was racing with what I didn't have and how fast could I get these things finished. My list for that particular day stemmed from being a little overwhelmed. Perhaps you can identify. We all have our own reality. But here's what I wrote down:

PROBLEMS:

    Car not working right

    Water in the basement

    Need software upgrade

You list the problem and then list the solution. No solution to a problem? There is always at least a piece of a problem that has a solution. Write that down.

The solutions I wrote for these annoyances were:

Car not working right	Drop the car at the mechanic
Water in the basement	Put the pump on in the basement
Need software upgrade	Just get the software update

Do the simplest things first to clear them off the list. Walking down into the basement is very easy. Easy to accomplish the hook-up of the pump, for a dry basement. (I was lucky I had one. If I didn't, it would be more complicated.) It really is the little stuff that accumulates to keep us stuck, and keeps us from going forward to have a good day. Throw a couple of good days together, and you're having a good week. Then a couple of good weeks together, and you're headed to a good life. No mystery here. So I took the car to the mechanic, and called a friend about what software I should buy. Events handled, stress reduced.

A fun list-keeping technique is one I do with friends around the holidays at the end of the year. This doesn't have to be done at New Year's, but prior to the new year is good. A small step to a fresh start. List what bad habits, bad situations, people with bad behavior you would like to be rid of. Yep! Be rid of. Situations that you would like cleared out. Gone!

Then write what you want to come into your life on another list. All the good things you would want. This is fun to do with other people. No one has to read your lists, unless you want to share. What do we do next? Take the list of "what you want to get rid of," and burn it. Then take the list of wishes or resolutions, or whatever and file them to read at the end of next year. Not everyone has file cabinets, so file them where you keep the holiday stuff. Here you know you will find them next year. It is amazing how you forget what you wrote, and what you have or haven't done to accomplish those wishes. More surprising, most times, is that what you wrote happens, and what you did accomplish is bigger than what you wished for.

If you are journalizing or keeping lists, what keeps showing up for you?

3

One Question, One Question Only

So far, we have been clearing our minds with exercise and listing desires. Now let us use our clearer minds to assist us in making decisions more quickly.

I am sure at times your mind can cloud the waters with a thousand reasons why you should or should not do something. Your mind may get stuck in a loop of indecision, pondering and pondering over something. Agonizing over something. This is immobilizing. Nothing gets done. No decision is made. No movement forward. To settle all those demons of indecision, I use the next technique as a real time saver.

This technique I call **"One Question, One Question Only."** Asking yourself one question, at a time, and ask so the answer is YES or NO. This simple technique eliminates that wasted time of pondering and agonizing.

In the start-up of any business, the owner usually does everything. Self-publishing my first book was indeed that way. I did the secretarial work, the selling and even the deliveries. I was busy. Not really enough time for pondering or agonizing, but I felt unsure if this was what I should be doing. The income did not equal the amount of time and effort that was going out. So I would ask myself one question. "Should I continue this?" YES or NO. I wasn't asking anyone else for input. Surely I would have been told to stop. Give up. I knew that. No, I was asking myself, "Should I continue this?" The answer would come back YES.

Now, where does this answer come from? It comes from a sense of knowing. A confident feeling of comfort with the initial answer. It is a comfort similar to the feeling when you had a multiple-choice test, and you put one answer down automatically. If later you doubted yourself and went back and changed it, usually you found out the first answer was the correct one. Same thing.

Let's practice. Is there something that you are waffling about? Indecisive about? Should I, or should I not? OK, sit still. No sips of coffee, no munching of food. No distractions.

Pose the question, so the answer has to be YES or NO.

NOW ask the question.

Should I move?

Should I start school next semester?

Should I stop seeing him/her?

Should I buy new sneakers?

Listen for the internal answer.

Is it a YES or a NO?

You have the answer.

Once you have that answer, proceed accordingly. Proceed with looking for a new house, getting those school catalogs, start to plan other activities without him/her or go to the store for new sneakers.

Do not second-guess yourself. Although there are some days you may have to ask yourself the same question every half hour, the more you use this technique you will learn to trust yourself with that first response. It doesn't matter whether the outside world is in line with that answer. The initial response is the way to proceed.

Sometimes we have difficult answers to face. Am I in the wrong work? Does he/she love me? The answers may be: YES, you're in the wrong work or NO, he/she doesn't love you. Not easy to hear, but your answers are never wrong, if you are following your values. Your values are the core beliefs of what is right or wrong for you.

I believe we can live with being unhappy for long lengths of time. However, we all have that instinct of knowing what particular level of unhappiness is not a natural state for us. There will be a constant whisper that we hear, or a feeling that something is not right. A nagging that says, " You can be." "You can do." "You are better than where you are." "Better than what you're putting up with."

Do you have something nagging at you? On the edges of your mind pulling at you? Things aren't right. Things aren't working. Something is missing. Something that needs attention. Use this technique for a clearer direction: Go through a list of life elements to figure out what it is that is nagging at you.

Is it the work? YES or NO.

Is it the family? YES or NO.

Is it your health? YES or NO.

Is it the marriage? YES or NO.

Is it your financial standing? YES or NO.

Is it the knot in your stomach or migraines that are a bother? YES or NO.

Is it not getting into that 2, 6, 10 or 14 comfortably? YES or NO.

Is it having too many commitments to your time? YES or NO.

Is it not being computer literate? YES or NO.

Is it not being happy? YES or NO.

Whatever your "it" is will assist you in pinning down the "what" that bothers you. Armed with YES or NO answers to the questions, you can then head in the direction of adjusting whatever the situation is. Too many commitments to your time? Start to delegate, or say no to things. Computer illiterate? Look into local computer courses. Ahh, the tough one of clothes too tight. No way around it but to diet and exercise. Jeez.

Another way to break through indecision with problem-solving is to ask yourself a question before you go to sleep. You may get the answer when you awake. Sounds easy? Not really! It will get easier when you are training the mind to do this. It takes practice. More importantly, it takes trusting yourself that indeed an answer will come. The answer may come in a dream, a feeling or a phrase. It may be there on waking from your sleep. Or it will come in the next day or two, in a chance meeting or event. It will come. Surprisingly, this seems to work even if you are under a lot of stress and have many decisions to make about something.

I can't say how this works, but it just does. A simple example of this technique is when I had to choose a logo for my company. I needed stationery and business cards. I knew I needed a logo. Why? Most companies I had worked with, or for, had a logo. So I thought I needed one. (Good thing I wasn't pondering a cafeteria. Where would I put it?) Anyway, I was under a time limit: I needed stationery to send out letters. And I didn't want the stationery printed without a logo. What would it be?

I had to go to the printer the next day with the logo, for the stationery to be printed. I asked myself that night, what will the logo look like? The next morning, I awoke with the image of me walking down a path carrying a lantern. In the dream, the time was night and the lantern was lighting the path ahead of me. I got up and drew the lantern.

If you look at the copyright page of this book, you will see the logo. The top is the handle of the lantern, the triangle the body and the lines are the light from the lantern. I am not an artist, but the look was there. It felt right. Thus the logo was found.

Your questions may not be about logos, or about what you are doing at your current work. Or they may be. Your questions will be specific to you, in your own timing. You may be looking for a YES or NO answer from "One Question, One Question Only." This answer will be immediate. Or you may need an answer with details, that takes a little while longer. Just ask yourself the question. I promise, you will get the answer.

4

Ask Ask Ask

So now you have the answers to YES or NO questions. Also, the answers to the questions with more details. Isn't this getting simpler and simpler? I hope so.

However, we may need some additional advice, when making a decision. This next technique is to ASK outside ourselves for something. Asking to see if something suits you, so you can confirm or redirect your decision.

Asking for something is hard, both asking ourselves or asking someone else. Does the difficulty of asking come from childhood? As a child, did you know the majority of things you would ask for would be denied? It became easier not to ask at all. We continue through life thinking we don't have permission to do something, to have something, or to try something. That if we asked, we would be told a resounding no. Some of us had the guilt of doing something without permission, and having the terror of getting caught. Getting caught doing something without permission meant getting punished.

However, I think by now most of us have all the

permission slips; we just don't use them. One of those permission slips is that we can ask for anything. We may still get a " NO." The point is we asked. And, just think, we might get a "YES."

Getting tied up in knots, afraid to ask, may be fear of the same resounding "NO" we received as kids. As an adult, the request is different but the feeling about asking seems to be the same. If I ask, I'll only hear a NO. I'll get the same feeling that NO brought on as a child. Maybe a feeling of not deserving.

A childhood of "No's" may be keeping you in an adulthood of nevers. You'll never do that. You'll never have that. You'll never achieve that. Remember, as children we had a small world of people to ask: our parents or guardians, family members, teachers or caretakers. Very little worldly contact. In this tiny world, those select few people were doing the best they could. As we grew taller, the world became larger, and so our world of asking took on grander possibilities.

Asking may be uncomfortable to you. It exposes you. If I ask for something, someone will know I want something that I don't have. That I am not complete at this time. So what? How can you complete what is missing, without going after it?

You can practice by asking other people for things. First do it by phone. If looking for work, call and ask if there are openings. No one can see you. The rejection is not personal. Ask for a sample newsletter in a profession you may want to be in. By phone, the people on the other end have never met you. They don't know what you look like. How old you are. That you cheat at cards. (Do you?)

Practice by phone. Do it in a quiet place, no music or TV on. Clear the area in your line of sight, except any notes you may have. This is a play. You have to rehearse your lines. Pick up the receiver, dial the number. Sit tall in the chair, head up, and clear your throat. "Hello. I would like to get information on, directions to, a free sample of." Whatever it may be. This practice, asking easy questions and shielded by the anonymity of the phone, is a wonderful way to build confidence. Then, you do the asking in person, again with a stranger, maybe in a department store or a restaurant. "May I have this? May I change that?" It is in the asking that you mold yourself to what you might want to be.

You may get what's not right for you. That is OK; you tried it. On to the next level of asking. Finding out what doesn't suit us brings us closer to what will. So venture out and ask for something. The asking is not just for life decisions, it's for comfort, too. For example, if on a business trip and staying in a hotel, ask for two beds. One bed becomes a desk on which to spread your work. The other you sleep in. This took me a couple of trips to figure out. The luxury of the king-sized bed, though wonderful, is not always practical for a work situation. Yes, there are desks in hotel rooms. They are just not big enough. Sounds like a simple request. It is, and it makes a world of difference lifting books or flyers off the bed vs. off the floor. Go for the comfort.

Let's say we need outside advice to decide about going into a certain field of work, or deciding to start your own business. Ask people who have their own businesses. Ask an expert in that field. How do you do that? You may have a friend who knows someone. This someone could ask for you. Or they could get you the OK to call, or meet that expert directly. You could use the Internet or the library for research. Then you could e-mail or write them. If it is a public figure, or business person at a large company, you may want to arrange an exploratory interview on their type of work. To meet with them you may call the personnel department at the company; if a public figure, call their staff and ask if this could be arranged.

Once you have contacted the expert, ask the person if he or she would mind answering some questions. If you write, ask if you can call or e-mail. If it's a phone call, have your questions ready. You may ask how they got started. What education or apprenticing was helpful. What is the reality of the work? What skills are needed? What is a typical day like? Do not waste the person's time by answering your own questions during this process. They'll think if you're such an expert, why are you seeking expert advice? Also, don't argue with the expert. You might want to say, "I didn't think things worked that way." If you don't agree, don't argue. Let it go.

You may find out you already know the information. You'll be thinking, "What was I so worried about, or blocked about? I now see how this is done." Talking to an expert takes away the mystery. I believe if another human has achieved something, I guess another human can do it. So why not you, right?

You could also use this technique of "ask the expert" when seeking a college, trade school, school system, new place of worship, or new hobby.

Let me stop right now to emphasize "ASKING" regarding a medical decision. The medical field is in an upheaval. We may have lost the trusted family physician to a corporate-designated provider listing. Not to say the doctors are not to be trusted, but possibly they will not be familiar with you and your family. With the HMO's, our doctors have to abide by many regulations. I believe the patient has suffered because of this.

For the best medical care, always go to a doctor's

appointment with your list of symptoms and questions you may have. Somehow even the smartest of us will get into a doctor's office and forget the questions and clam up. A good one is, "Boy, is the doctor busy! I'd better not ask him too many questions." One reason he is busy is because people didn't ask him questions in the first place. Another good one is, "I will be bothering him. He may think I am dumb." Medicine is a business like any other. You pay for a service, you deserve the best treatment that you are paying for. You deserve to be treated with respect. We all did not go to medical school. They did. So they should share what they know. And they will, if you ask. If you do not get an answer, keep asking. If a particular doctor is not answering, ask for a different doctor. And keep asking.

If, after whatever treatment is given, you still do not feel better, keep asking. Ask for a second opinion, or another referral, or to see a specialist. Also, ask another patient or a friend. "What do you think I should ask the doctor? What questions have I left out?" If you are the patient, you most likely are under a lot of stress.

You will need to get the questions in order, prior to all visits.

You may not be asking for yourself but for a family member, a friend, or a child. The medical practices are overwhelmed. They are human. Their time is limited. Yours may be too, if you don't ask.

All right already, enough of that. Oh, I can go on in this department. KEEP ASKING. ASK! ASK! ASK!

A more gentle place for advice is to ask a friend. I am sure you know who they are. They are the trusted ones. A friend, when asked, will give you the advice of a mirror. The clear picture of what is. I'm sure, like my friends, your friends are better at some things than you are. So ask them their opinion. Also, the dearest of friends know you, what you like and dislike. The truest of friends know what is best for you. Here is an arena of asking that will keep you grounded and steady.

Lastly or firstly (your choice), you ask God or who-ever "God" may be to you. Maybe you ask your angels.

Whatever it is outside yourself that you may pray to, just ask. Now, with all the other input suggested above, you will have more facts, more details, and some answers to make the best decisions to go in the right direction.

Ask for a better life, better work, better relationships. You may see people and it appears they have it all. I bet they got half by asking for it, and worked hard for the rest. I also think we need to ask for opportunity. Ask to volunteer at something you might want to work at, ask for the next new project to expand your skills, ask for more time to yourself, ask for more time with people you love, ask for the best: view, seat, window, room, office, food, table, haircut, life.

This world is ours for the asking. In fact, it is ours until we are unable to ask anymore. So, go ahead, ask for something now. For yourself. For your comfort. For your personal growth. For your financial future. For your family. For a friend. For your happiness. For the heck of it. ASK.

5

See it to Be it

Athletes do it, actresses and actors do it and those who are healing do it. Do what? They envision themselves as Olympic winners, Oscar winners or healthy. This envisioning is called visualization. Visualization is a technique that can assist with the adjustment of someone's view of life. This different view works to modify the reality.

Experts in the field of stress management utilize visualization techniques. When a person is in a stressful situation, it is recommended to see oneself in a calm place, to take themselves on a mini-vacation in their mind. Thinking themselves to be in a calm place makes for a calmer person. This calmer person is able to handle the present stressful situation better.

Another example: as a child, did you have nightmares and the adults around you told you to think of something pleasant, so you wouldn't be scared? Same technique, except now we are a little taller. So why not pretend in your mind to be a happy adult, making quality decisions. If you're not one in real-life already. What a dilemma at this point! Sometimes we are digging deep for the right answers with asking. Other times we are visualizing the right situations. Some busy days ahead.

Visualization is taking the moment to see in your mind's eye, what you would like to achieve. How do you see yourself to be? A happier you, a better position, deleting negative behavior or living well?

At times, we don't or can't see what it is that would be better. However, we know the present is just not what we want. If this is your case, just hang in there as you start any process. Write it out. Ask. Do visualization. What is missing will surface, to be attended to.

I believe we should teach these practices in schools. Have our children know that there is no real mystery in believing you can do anything. Seeing is believing. In the believing, begins the achieving.

Career counselors use this in assisting clients to see themselves getting work. They have their clients see in their mind's eye how they will get to the interview, how they will be dressed, how they will be calmly sitting waiting to go into the final interview. How calm they will be when answering the questions on the interview. This could be done as a guided imagery, with the client sitting with their eyes closed and the counselor walking through the process of the interview. Have them imagine getting the position and accepting the job. They often suggest a client do this for themselves the night before the interview, or first thing when they get up. Mentally rehearse on the way to the interview. Seeing themselves calm, collected and on. Visualizing receiving the call, or letter, that congratulates the candidate and says, "Come work with us."

What is great about visualization: it is free, there is no age range, no calories, it can be done anywhere, at any time. It can be accomplished by anyone no matter what race, creed, marital status, gender or religion. There is no waiting until you get a better job, or have a husband/wife, or divorce one, or get a new home or have children. It starts right now. It is always the right time to be cooking up what you would like your life to be. Even though nothing is moving, it seems your mind starts the cataloging. Then your reality meets up with your mind. Another tool for the rest of your life.

Visualization becomes a habit. As you visualize, you see results you can't help but to continue to practice. What your mind thinks of yourself, is what you become.

OK, you think you have nothing to visualize? Can't grasp the concept? Think of yourself in a place you love to be. A comfortable chair, couch, a favorite spot in your home. Maybe right now it is not in your home, which may be chaotic. Where is your slice of peace? Think of it. It will make you feel peaceful. (There's that mind and body connection working again.) The feeling of peace is the same for all of us. Only the places differ.

Now go a step further. If you can see in your mind something with which you are familiar and comfortable, why not visualize a place you have never been, but believe you belong there? You can visualize a piece of the picture. Let's say you dislike your current work. Visualize a different environment, one in which you feel more comfortable. Once you start to see in your mind's eye what you may want, the steps to get you out of the current work become more clear. You begin to change your attitude. You begin to be a nicer person at your present work. The nicer you creates the next opportunity. The nicer you starts to reach out to where you belong. Your reality will catch up with your mind.

There will always be refinements of any situation that exists. Some are livable and easily adjusted and forgotten. Some must be attended to daily. We could possibility "think" off the ten pounds, but that doesn't work by itself. I wish it did. What does work is if you visualize a thinner self, and how your clothes will fit, when it comes time to exercise you won't fight it as much. You'll just do it. When faced with the delicious dreaded basket of bread when out to dinner, let me be unkind here, you won't hog down. What you think about will enforce your behavior, to get to your goals. However, I do recommend this: never travel without a rubber band for that expanding waistline.

OK, you are trying this, and nothing seems to be

happening. If there is any doubt at all, nothing will happen. The doubt cancels out the process. If you don't believe, you won't achieve. You must cultivate the will of personal belief. This is a tough one. All of us have different levels of childhood mistreatments, longings or missing pieces. Those scars of childhood may keep us back from believing in ourselves. This subject would be a book in itself. However, once recognized that healing needs to be done with the past, awareness will set in motion a healing process in the present.

This life is your canvas. No matter how bleak, filled with disappointment or overwhelmed your current life may be, you can make the adjustments toward a more peaceful life. Some situations really don't get better by us worrying about them. One technique with worry is to visualize putting it away. Let's do this together. You have a problem you can't solve at this moment. Let us visualize putting the problem away in a box. See yourself possibly taping the box shut. Opening a closet door, putting the worry box on the shelf in a closet. Now close the door. Maybe even lock the door. This process discontinues the looping of the problem in your head. It is the permission to let go. To stop the looping. To let the situation take care of itself. To rid ourselves of the going round and round with an issue. If you put worry in a box, in a closet, and shut the door, you can't get to it. Funny thing–the situation does take care of itself. This is a process of taking your mind off something. Leaving it alone. Getting out of your own way. Visualization can be the coming and the going of things. You say, "How can I do this? I have to attend to this!" Do you? Is it draining you daily? You can put things away for a half hour, if it relieves you of worry. When you get good at this, maybe you can put something away for a lifetime. It's there, but it is in the closet. Try it. Put worry away in this perceived place for an hour, for a day or forever.

Another worry technique is to put a time limit on it. In any new business you may experience money crunches. For example, you may need so much money to pay vendors on Friday. Here it is Monday, with a lack of funds. Begin to think that there is a solid week of unlimited funding possibilities. Say to yourself, "Not to worry on Monday, keep your head down and keep working." By Friday the solution will happen. It always does.

To receive some assistance with visualization, you could listen to tapes on guided imagery. Sounds good, but here enters one of life's trickeries. You may say, "OK, I am ready to do this, but I need some outside assistance." You go to the store or the library, and get a tape on visualization. You can't wait to start. You have your time set aside, the place set up, you put the tape on, adjust the volume and the voice starts. You can't stand the sound of the person's voice. At this point you say, "Boy, this is stupid. I don't like it. I don't get it. I can't do this." Return the tape. Get another one. We are all so different. Find the voice, or style, you are comfortable with.

Another great thing about visualization is there is no wrong or right way to do this. You can't fail. You can only gain. You may not be able to grasp the entire situation that will make your current life better, but you could visualize a part of the puzzle. Let's say you want a more casual workplace. Visualize yourself leaving for this new work in casual clothes. You don't know what the work is, but you are preparing yourself for the future. Or visualize a day without pain, be it physical or mental. What do those days look like?

This "seeing in one's mind" assists us with being comfortable with our futures. If you visualize what you believe you deserve, then when you begin to live the reality, you will be comfortable there. It is our belief in ourselves that creates the opportunity, where none exists in the present. Does this visualization, being a positive thing, create positive hormones or brain waves that assist in goal achieving? I don't know, but there is that body and mind connection. Where the mind goes, the body will follow.

Begin right now wherever you are. Working or not working. Happy or not. Healthy or not. Begin visualizing how you want your world to turn. Creating that positive antenna for you. The creations are limitless. What can stand in your way? Only you can envision where and what you want to be. Go ahead, see it to be it.

6

The Days
of Doubt

No matter what your decisions will be or how you follow them, having done all the research, you will have Days of Doubt, fondly termed the "D days." They will come. It is almost as if they happen to test you a little. Those days are asking you, "Are you really sure you made the right decision?"

The "D days" are filled with calamities of things going wrong, or things not happening in your time frame. They attempt to cloud your vision. To get in the way of your process and progress. These days test your sanity, to see if you are going to proceed with the commitment to that great new idea, or product, or new book, or new career, or new move, or life-style change, or treatment.

In the beginning, with the newness of something, there will be many "D days." As your decisions become more focused, there will be fewer. However, they still will come.

I was invited to Washington, D.C. to be a part of a conference on training. I was honored to have been invited. I printed an additional 5,000 copies of my first book. I didn't know, mind you, the nature of a book-selling sales cycle yet. I was new to this. I received the shipment of books and put them on my back porch, fondly known as the K-Slaw, Inc. book depository. Now the porch is closed in, but not heated. It was the winter of the numerous snow storms and government closings. The conference was canceled. May I say, I felt I was being tested. Those books sat on that porch for months as I built my business. I believed they were laughing at me. In addition, books and weather changes do not mix. As I would open each carton, there was a layer of books that were buckled due to the weather changes. These books had to be replaced and the boxes repacked. OK, not a life-threatening situation, but not a wise business decision. This decision caused me many a "D day."

Once recognized, the "D days" are seen as nothing more than a roadside stop. A brief time-out. Once admitted, once conquered. Easy? Never. They keep you humble. Just accept the process of a decision. The process may create new directions which will have some obstacles, that's all.

You will doubt yourself. That's one thing, but when other people are doubting you, well, that is something else. These usually are the same people who say they are worried about you. Don't you just love that? You meet someone and they say, "Gee, I worry about you." You're thinking, "I thought everything was fine." Usually they don't have all the facts. Let it go. You know who these people are. Just read their name tags: "Hi, my name is _____ and I am here to doubt you, and to tell you I worry about you. I represent any doubt you harbor in yourself. I will shatter any belief you may have in yourself." Usually when people doubt us, we get angry and frustrated with trying to explain ourselves. We know that to explain oneself is the wrong thing to do. How many times have we all seen that trap ahead and just walked into it? Try not to waste energy with explaining, and just keep moving forward. Sometimes from this frustration, we obtain that wonderful "just-watch-me energy" that fuels us on to the next project.

On the "D days," you really have to put your hand in the bag of tricks and pull out what will make you centered again. Get up, go out and take a walk, call a friend or just cry. The "D day" is almost over, and tomorrow is always better.

You may have a bad day, no matter what your choices are. Just call it a "D day."

7

Jump

OK, we have been walking, writing, asking, and visualizing. Maybe not all at the same time, but a walk with a dear friend asking them some questions bundles a couple of techniques. Very nice. We have gathered the facts, weighed the data in our minds and now we must JUMP.

Yep, there comes a time to just begin. To take the one step forward. To start. To jump in. The basis for success is movement. The starting of any little routine that makes a difference in your work, social life, your weight, your children, your relationships, your health. Without movement, things do not change or get attended to.

There may be a part of you that says, "It is too late for me to make a jump. My opportunities are over. I have too many responsibilities." Valid statements to be considered, but do they carry an unrealistic weight? Does this self-perception keep you safe so you don't jump at all? So you never begin anything new? Again, a lot easier not to jump than to stay stuck. Maybe you think you have had a missed opportunity in your past? Whatever stumbles, missed opportunities, heartaches, business failings, illnesses, financial disasters or firings you have had are situations that assist you toward the way you want to be treated. These situations guide you to the way you want to live now.

"Jump" may be too much of an action word. Some of our decisions may not need such a dramatic action. For example, the jump into a diet. The action of moment-to-moment dietary choices has a very clear outcome, yet not a dramatic action. If we choose to eat an apple every day, or a slice of apple pie, what will the outcome be in a month's time? Most of us, if we chose the pie, would look like a pear. A moment's decision to eat or not to eat. Not a great action in the moment but, over time, produces dramatic results.

You may not want to announce to the world the timing of your jump. This will save you from listening to endless questions from others if you never jump, or if you do, and do not have a soft landing. You do not need to hear, "You can't do that." Some people will attempt to stomp on your dreams—not step, stomp. Basically they may be afraid you will change, or they may have to change. They may feel insecure that you may become smarter than they. You may leave them. How frightening and threatening. Just continue forward. The true people will always remain. If you keep your jump silent, code it on a calendar. Seeing it daily may assist with the reality of the jump.

There are times we feel we are alone in this process of exploration. You may have lots of people in your life, but are alone in this "newness" of venturing out into the unfamiliar. Lots of people have gone before you in their self-exploration. This aloneness, I believe, is to have us find the tools that are not a carbon copy of anyone else's. The road traveled alone while reinventing yourself is traveled quicker. This time is not forever. Thank goodness. Again, the real friends will remain.

At this point, it all sounds good. You may be saying, "I wish I could do that." Start something towards a goal. Nothing will happen without a "JUMP." The reaching out, the stretching, the attempt, and now this jump.

The timing of the actual jump from decision to action may be in 15 minutes or 15 years. We live in our personal preparation moment to moment. It's almost like we are always preparing our launch silently. The point is: there is a jump. The jump is the difference of having or not having, of achieving or not. The jump is the first step in the unknown. It could be as small as a simple phone call to ask for something, or as big as quitting your job to begin a new one.

You could "jump" by volunteering first at something, before you totally give up the day job or invest any money. Invest a little time. Say you made the decision, "OK, I will buy a franchise." Go volunteer, or work in one part-time. This counts as a jump. It is movement to find out if you like it. Do you like the smell of the place? Do you like the type of people who work there? Do you like the customers? You should find out for yourself. This may also be done privately. So as to not hear, "What would so-and-so say if they see you working in _____." Statements that may sting you, or assist you in doubting yourself, or stopping yourself. If the big "THEY" ride by, or come in, and see you wearing a hairnet and a name tag, just wave. This is your life to figure out. If by chance this jump begets a string of franchises, who is the smart one?

Sometimes we are faced with a jump. No choice. No place to go. We have to jump. Have to make a decision. Have to face up and take a swing. An example of an unexpected learning jump happened during my radio show, "Workline." About six months into doing a show at a small station in New Jersey, there was a blizzard during my time slot. I called the station and said, "I can't make it in because of the weather. Can you run an old show tape?" Their regular engineer was not in and the new person couldn't find my tapes. She said,

"You can go on live from your home, or we will run a different show." She put me on hold. You have been in this situation, faced with yourself. What do I do now? OK, I have never done this. Other people (other people with years of experience) do radio shows from their home. When am I going to learn this skill? On a major station? I don't think so. Wouldn't it be better to learn in this environment, with maybe fewer listeners? I wanted the comfort of a face-to-face engineer to assist me. This was not a life-threatening decision. How many really are? Yet, I was paralyzed with fear.

She came back on the line, and said, "What are you going to do"? I said, "Let's do the show from home." I did have time to set up my office. Phone and notes in front of me, with a clock and wristwatch with a second hand to keep track of the time and commercial breaks. I was ready as I was going to be. Nervous, but ready. The noon news was over, and I was on the air. Everything was going along just fine. My voice became stronger. I made the first commercial break fine. The snow is coming down fast. I am cocooned in my office. The show was going well. Then the doorbell rang. I am on the air. I am on the air live, but I am also the "block watch captain" in my neighborhood. (No uniform, no badges.) What if one of the elderly neighbors has a problem? I have to answer the door, but I am on the air live. On a phone that is stationary. OK, what do I do? I dragged the phone to the door and told the audience, whatever listeners there were, that we were going to answer the door together. The phone cord was stretched to a hair. I answered the door. There stood two very young little boys with their shovels taller than they. They came to ask if they could shovel my driveway. I was expecting a neighbor in trouble. After the initial shock: "How could their mothers let them out in a blizzard?" I told them to come back later. They did. The show went on to a fine finish. I had jumped, and the landing had been met with only brief anguish.

The jump is the commitment to oneself to do something different. To change a poor situation for the better. To learn something new. To stretch oneself. To begin going in a new direction. To alter the present. To attempt something new. To jump into the life you are deciding for yourself.

8

The Timing of Things

There is no mistake with the timing of things: the initiating of a decision, or the timing of the outcome of that decision.

Let's say you had made a decision to begin something new, and it seems like there is a waiting time to it. You seem to be hitting a brick wall, or what you think are unnecessary obstacles. This is frustrating. We usually see the reason for the wait sometime afterward. Better opportunities may present themselves during that waiting time. You may have experienced this type of timing glitch. You put yourself under the pressure of a deadline. The deadline is not met for a number of reasons. Those reasons become clear sometime later.

There are also decisions that you make, that turn out not to be the best in time. A past decision is not working in the present. We may have clicked off the college program for a certain major, go through school, graduate, and not like it. You now have to re-examine the choice, and proceed with new decisions for a new direction. However, nothing is lost with the first decision.

If it was an educational choice, the education will be applied in some way. With your health, you may choose to proceed with a procedure or mode of treatment, and then decide it does not work for you. You can change it. This is the best time in life to be flexible. You can change your decisions. Things are not so black and white. Differences are acceptable. It is your decision to choose where you belong, with the variety of choices. We all work with the best tools we know at the time. Some additional tools come with the wisdom of age and experience, or both.

I believe there is the magic and rewards with making a decision. We see this often with love. A person makes the decision to break an engagement because things aren't right, and meets someone more suitable soon after. An uncomfortable decision made is rewarded in time—by true love perhaps?

With the awareness of the timing of things, you get an understanding. Comfort comes with the process of time. Let's say you are thinking about moving. You can't decide if it is a good thing. Then you get some new neighbors that are not so nice, or your lease is up. These events contribute to the decision. Same thing happens with work. You can't decide when to make a change, then you get a monster boss. The nutty neighbors or bad bosses assist you to move forward, to find what is best for you. This timing of outside influences helps you to process quickly a decision not yet acted upon.

It is always OK to say to someone, "I can't decide today. I have to get back to you on that." Whatever the issue. This gives you the time to employ the mentioned techniques, to gather more data. To possibly sit still with the question, and wait to feel what comfort level you have with the answer. Or sleep on it. How do you feel about the question first thing in the morning?

When you get really good at this, you will feel confident. I don't know how I feel now about making this decision, but if I let it go and wait, I'll know the answer tomorrow, or in a week, or even an hour from now. This is the concept of knowing that all the right answers and situations come in the right time. It cuts down on a bit of the anxiety, when we think things aren't going fast enough or happening soon enough.

Be patient with time, for it will present added direction to your decisions. Call it a timing thing. It always is.

9

Befriend Yourself

self, you know what may make you happy during times of stress with indecision. This does not have to do with money. Yes, it would be great to jump on a plane and change the current location in a whim: a beachfront room somewhere, or that secluded cabin on the lake where you can take a break and relax. Whatever your fantasy preference. For most of us, it is not real life. What is real always is daily living. What you do daily, that creates who you are, and how you live, and how you care for yourself.

Do a task that is simplistic, that needs doing. You'll find finishing the task triggers that feeling of accomplishment. This process assists you to get ready for that same feeling, when the big accomplishments happen. I find one of the best tasks is to clear out clutter. A mindless task of clearing out creates space to have the new come in. Other simplistic tasks may include doing the laundry, cooking, baking, paying bills, fixing something, washing the car. Whatever it is that is simple, and you feel a sense of accomplishment when it is completed.

There may be times that simply sitting still is the

answer. Use meditation to quiet the time of indecision. You can meditate on asking yourself a question, and then silently sit and wait for an answer. There are many forms of meditation. One way to meditate is to concentrate on one word or phrase, repeated over and over silently. You can create peace and silence by sitting some extra minutes quietly, before you go into work or before going into your home. To settle yourself. At work, escape to that bathroom stall for a moment of peace. Don't laugh; but laugh if you must. It may be the only peaceful place you can find in the day. Make it work. I just love the magazines that show people meditating by a beautiful stream on a mountainside. Where is that place? That mountainside stream may not be accessible in your daily life. Make what is around you work. Maybe find a place of worship that is open at lunch time, and sit in prayer and silence. You could also do a guided meditation that does take you to the beachfront resort or lake cabin in your mind. Meditation can be as simple as mindful deep breathing. Take a few deep breaths, then go on to the next challenge, question, situation or person.

You may have to step back and take a look at the big picture, so that you can see how your decisions are progressing towards that better future. For instance, every time you choose that apple, instead of a slice of apple pie, you win a small weight victory for yourself. Every time you finish that one page of a manuscript, you are closer to that finished novel. Every time you visit the library to do research, you are one step closer to the knowledge you need for the next new venture. Every sit-up gets you closer to that flatter belly. The daily choices create the future successes.

Befriend yourself. Only you know what it is that is best for you. What would you take out of your bag of tricks? Would a walk work, a call to a friend, an hour of couch-time, go to a movie, a nap even? What is it that will keep you centered?

We seem to be tested when we start something new. It is almost as if the testing starts to try and stop your progress, and good work. You will have "D days," and timing things will happen. You have known these people: if they just hung in there a little longer, not given up, they would have gotten what they wanted. They gave up too soon. They may say, "This doesn't work. I don't deserve this." They listen to the disapproval from other people. If you are experiencing any of these hurdles, take a short break. Then dive back into the techniques of walking, praying, writing, asking, visualizing and listening to yourself. I promise you, the time will pass and a more clear direction will appear.

At what time do you give up? When your gut tells you. If you still waffle over something, when in doubt, don't. The point is to befriend yourself, to be able to listen to yourself, to do what is best at the time, and proceed.

Sometimes it is to walk away. Sometimes it is to change your attitude toward the situation, and continue. It is in you to know what is best for you. What tools work today may not work tomorrow, but may the day after. Know that our decisions are not cut in stone, but are flowing in progress for the best life possible at the given time.

Another kindness thought for oneself: No matter

how successful, happy or together someone appears, they had to start somewhere, to practice towards that great success. They had to have stumbled, maybe even fallen, but they continued on. During your stumbles, choose not to quit, but to carry on. We all have stumbled in the past. We know how, and when, and why. Forgive yourself of the past, and carry on, choosing things to be proud of in the present.

As a friend to ourselves, we can laugh with ourselves and at ourselves. Which brings me to the point of humor. Got to have it. When those brain cells are burning with indecision, call those friends you laugh with the most. And laugh. Nothing better than friends laughing, laughing at yourself, children laughing or your partner laughing with you.

Knowing yourself is also knowing places and people that keep you safe. Knowing yourself is knowing when to rest. Knowing yourself is knowing who should not be in your life any longer. Knowing yourself is understanding (in good time) the answers to your questions will appear.

When you have made your decisions and set yourself in new directions, guess what? There will be all sorts of new decisions, and new situations to decide upon. However, now they will be made more smoothly, with confidence, having made a decision at all.

You Decide.

About the Author

Karen Okulicz is the author of "Try! A Survival Guide to Unemployment." Try! is a utilized resource by state and federal programs, outplacement firms, in military RIFs and spouse programs. Try! is listed on the Self Publishers Hall of Fame. Ms. Okulicz is a continual guest on radio and TV. She has led numerous workshops at Workforce Conferences nationally. Ms. Okulicz has hosted and produced the radio show "Workline."

It has taken her approximately six years to decide to publish her second book, "Decide! How to make any decision."

ORDER FORM

Order online www.GUIDESFORYOU.com or fax to 732-681-1318
Mail: Checks payable to K-Slaw, Inc., P.O. Box 375, Belmar, NJ 07719

	Amount	Price	Total
"Try!" A Survival Guide to Unemployment	_____ X _____		_____
"Decide!" How to make any Decision	_____ X _____		_____
"Attitude!" For your best lived life	_____ X _____		_____

Please add 6% Tax for NJ only _____

Shipping \$15.00 per box of 100 books   Shipping and Handling   _____
Purchase order # _____   TOTAL   _____

Bulk Discount 1-10 \$10.00 per book, 11 to 99 \$6.00 per book, 100 to 999 \$5.00 per book,
1000 to 4,999 \$3.00 per book and over 5,000 \$2.50 per book.
Books can be mixed for the best discount!

Call 1-888-529-6090 • Fax 732-681-1318 • Email Karen@guidesforyou.com
Visa and Mastercard Accepted.

Ship to: Name _____ Title _____

Organization _____

Address _____

City _____ State _____ ZIP _____

Phone# _____ Fax _____

Email _____

CALL FOR GSA RATES GSA# GS-02F-1410H • TAX ID# 223325968

THANK YOU!